Ramen Cookbook

50 Ramen Recipes for the Home Chef

BY

Julia Chiles

Copyright 2020 - Julia Chiles

License Notes

No part of this Book can be reproduced in any form or by any means including print, electronic, scanning or photocopying unless prior permission is granted by the author.

All ideas, suggestions and guidelines mentioned here are written for informative purposes. While the author has taken every possible step to ensure accuracy, all readers are advised to follow information at their own risk. The author cannot be held responsible for personal and/or commercial damages in case of misinterpreting and misunderstanding any part of this Book

Table of Contents

Introduction... 6

Black bean Fajita Ramen.. 7

Steak, Broccoli, & Ramen... 9

Cajun Shrimp Ramen... 11

Spicy Red Pepper Tofu Ramen... 13

Andouille Ramen... 15

BLT Ramen Bowl.. 17

BLT Avocado Pineapple Salsa Ramen Bowl................................... 19

Italian Ramen Chowder.. 21

Sweet Potatoes Pork Ramen... 23

Chicken Sun-Dried Tomatoes... 25

Gumbo Ramen Medley.. 27

Shrimp Okra Ramen Bowl... 29

Cheesy Ham and Ramen... 31

Queso with Chicken Ramen... 33

Ramen Steak and Broccoli... 35

Artic Ranch Ramen with Andouille 37

Southern Stew 39

Ramen Ragu 41

Creamy Chicken Ramen.. 43

Chicken Mojo Ramen.. 45

Black Bean and Tomato on a Bed of Ramen 47

Turkey Ramen Stew 49

Vegetarian Ramen Italian Veggies.. 51

Spicy Italian Sausage Ramen Bowl 53

Kielbasa and Sauerkraut.. 55

Italian Sausage Ramen Bowl... 57

Ramen Kimchi Soup 59

Tomato and Eggplant Ramen... 61

Kimchi with Ramen 63

Spicy Herb Ramen 65

Turkey Stew 67

Onion Soup... 69

Apple Chops on a Bed of Ramen 71

Pork Carnita on a Bed of Ramen 73

Beef Carnita on a Bed of Ramen 75

Ramen Beef Stew 77

Gluten Free Chicken with Spring Onion Ramen 79

Sauerkraut and Kielbasa 81

Creamy Chicken with Tortillas 83

Easy Chicken Fajita Ramen 85

Ramen Enchilada 87

Salsa Ramen 89

Beef Au Jus with Ramen 91

Chicken Ramen Soup 93

Peppers and Ginger Ramen 95

Greek Ramen 97

Cod Ramen 99

Ramen with Scallops 101

Hot Smoky Shrimp Ramen 103

Italian Ramen Ragu 105

Author's Afterthoughts 107

Introduction

Liven up dinner and lunch! Wake up that tired old recipe with some delicious ramen recipes! Take a meal to the next level with 50 great ramen recipes for every occasion.

Things to Know About This Cookbook…

Unless specifically stated, do not use seasoning packet!

Black bean Fajita Ramen

Use ground beef in a pinch! Makes 2 servings

Ingredients:

- 1 cup ramen noodles
- ½ cup strips of steak or chicken strips
- 1/2 packet no sodium taco seasoning or fajita seasoning (such as Mrs. Dash)
- ¼ cup low sodium pineapple salsa
- ½ cup low-sodium black beans, washed & drained
- 1/2 cup worth julienned onions and bell peppers
- 2-3 cups low sodium beef broth

Instructions:

In medium size pot warm onions and pepper 30-45 seconds.

Stir in protein, seasoning, salsa, black beans, broth.

Bring to boil, reduce heat, cover, let simmer 8-9 minutes.

Steak, Broccoli, & Ramen

Let the meat come to room temperature before cooking! Makes 2 servings

Ingredients:

- ¼ tablespoon olive oil
- 1 cup of diced steak
- ½ Tbsp beef bouillon paste (we use Better Than Bullion Beef)
- 4-6 broccoli trees
- ½ tsp Italian seasoning
- 1/2 cup no salt added crushed tomatoes
- 1 package ramen noodles
- 3 cups low sodium beef or vegetable broth

Instructions:

In pot warmed over medium high heat, oil, steak, and bullion paste. Sauté steak & broccoli 45 seconds or until all is brown.

Add in seasoning, tomatoes, ramen, broth.

Bring to a boil, reduce heat, cover, let simmer 8-9 minutes

Cajun Shrimp Ramen

Serve with toasted baguettes! Makes 2 servings

Ingredients:

- 1 tablespoon olive oil
- 1 tsp no salt Cajun seasoning
- 1 shallot diced
- 1 clove garlic grated
- 1 bell pepper diced -or- 1 diced jalapeno
- ¼-1/3 cup low sodium diced tomato
- 1 avocado diced
- ½ cup andouille sausage
- 1 can low sodium black beans washed and drained
- 1 cup shredded Monterey jack cheese
- 1 package ramen noodles (w/o seasoning)
- 2 cups beef broth

Instructions:

In a pot or skillet with high sides bring to heat over a burner set for med-high heat; add oil, shallot, garlic, pepper, seasoning and sauté 1 minute.

Add in tomatoes, avocado, sausage, beans, cheese, noodles, broth.

Bring to a boil, reduce heat, cover, let simmer 8-9 minutes.

Spicy Red Pepper Tofu Ramen

A great vegetarian meal! Makes 2 servings

Ingredients:

- 1/4 cup baby ears of corn
- 2 tbsp diced water chestnut
- 2-4 drops chili oil
- 1/3 cup worth purple cabbage or Kim chi
- 1 cup roasted red pepper low-sodium broth
- 1/4 block silken cubed tofu
- ½ tsp minced garlic
- 1 package ramen noodles (w/o seasoning)

Instructions:

In pot warmed over medium high heat add corn, chestnuts, oil, Kim chi, broth, garlic, tofu.

Bring to a boil, reduce heat, cover, let simmer 8-9 minutes

Andouille Ramen

Try with kale! Makes 2 servings

Ingredients:

- 1 tbsp olive oil
- 1 link andouille sausage diced
- 1 cup spinach chopped
- 1/4 cup diced black olives
- Juice of ½ lime
- 1/3 cup salsa
- 1 cup shredded Monterey jack cheese
- 1 package ramen noodles
- 1/3 cup low sodium beef broth

Instructions:

Pour oil in pot warmed over hi heat then sauté sausage 45 seconds to 1 min.

Add in spinach, olives, lime juice, salsa stirring 45 seconds to 1 minute before

Add in ramen noodles and toss.

Pour in broth and stir well.

Bring to a boil, reduce heat, cover, let simmer 5 minutes.

BLT Ramen Bowl

For extra crunch, add walnuts or pine nuts! Makes 2 servings

Ingredients:

- 1 cup ramen noodles cooked as directed, divided
- 1/3 cup crumbled bacon, divided
- 8 cherry tomatoes, divided
- 2 romaine lettuce leaves, divided
- 2 tablespoons mango salsa, divided
- 1/3 cup crumbled feta cheese, divided

Instructions:

Layout lettuce leaves and fill both with ½ cup cooked ramen noodles.

Top each with ½ bacon and tomatoes.

Top each with salsa.

Top each with feta cheese.

BLT Avocado Pineapple Salsa Ramen Bowl

Great for lunch! Makes 2 serving

Ingredients:

- 1 package ramen noodles cooked as directed
- ¼ cup crumbled bacon, divided
- 1/4 cup diced tomato, divided
- 2 romaine lettuce leaves
- 1/3 cup avocado diced, divided
- 2 tablespoons pineapple salsa, divided
- 2 Tbsp parsley or thyme

Instructions:

Layout lettuce leaves and fill both with ½ cup cooked ramen noodles.

Top each with ½ bacon, tomatoes, avocados.

Top each with salsa.

Top each with parsley or thyme.

Italian Ramen Chowder

Try it with Greek Seasoning! Makes 2 servings

Ingredients:

- 1 Tbsp canola oil
- 1 Tbsp minced onion
- 1 tsp minced garlic
- 2/3 cup ground beef
- 1/2 cup edamame
- 1 tablespoon diced black olives
- 1 tsp Greek seasoning
- 1 cup shredded mozzarella cheese
- 1/2 Tbsp diced oregano
- 1 package ramen
- 1 1/4 cups low-sodium beef broth

Instructions:

Brown ground beef and drain.

In pot or high walled skillet pour in oil, onion, and garlic; sauté 1 minute.

Stir in ground beef edamame, ramen, broth.

Bring to a boil, reduce heat, cover, let simmer 8-9 minutes; fix two bowls and top each with cheese and parsley.

Sweet Potatoes Pork Ramen

Add turmeric or ginger! Makes 2 servings

Ingredients:

- 1 Tablespoon butter
- 1 diced shallot
- Olive oil spray
- 1 cup sweet potato cubes
- 1 tsp smoked paprika
- ½ cup ground pork, cooked
- 1 package ramen, cooked

Instructions:

Preheat oven to 400 and line baking sheet with aluminum foil sprayed with olive oil.

Spread out potato cubes, sprinkle with smoked paprika and mist lightly with oil spray.

Mix cooled potatoes with cooked pork and cooked ramen.

Chicken Sun-Dried Tomatoes

Also great with bell pepper broth! Makes 2 servings

Ingredients:

- 3 Tbsp butter
- ¼ cup onions julienned
- 1/3 cup shredded chicken
- 1 cup Tuscan sun-dried tomato broth
- 1 cup macadamia nuts
- 1 package ramen
- 1/2 teaspoon oregano chopped divided
- ½ teaspoon rosemary

Instructions:

In pot over med-high heat melt butter and sauté onions 5 minutes.

Add in shredded chicken, macadamia nuts, ramen, broth.

Bring to a boil, reduce heat, cover, let simmer 8-9 minutes.

Ladle into two bowls; top with oregano and rosemary.

Gumbo Ramen Medley

Try it with seafood! Makes 2 servings

Ingredients:

- ½ Tbsp olive oil
- 1/3 onion diced
- 1/2 teaspoon minced garlic
- Juice of 1 lime
- 1 spoonful chicken bouillon paste (we used Better Then Bouillon
- 1/3 cup shredded chicken
- 1/3 cup low sodium chickpeas or garbanzo beans
- 2/3 cup baby spinach leaves
- 1/3 cup tomatoes, quartered
- ½ cup low sodium chicken broth

Instructions:

In pot warmed over medium high pour in olive oil then add onion and garlic and let sauté 1 minute.

Stir in juice of lime, bouillon paste, and shredded chicken and cook 1 minute.

Add in spinach, tomatoes, chicken broth.

Bring to boil, reduce temp, cover, let simmer 5-7 minutes.

Shrimp Okra Ramen Bowl

Try it vegetarian! Servings 2.

Ingredients:

- 1/3 Tbsp olive oil
- 1 chopped shallot
- 1 clove garlic chopped
- 1/2 cup whole kernel corn
- 1/3 cup okra
- ¼ cup edamame
- 2 Tbsp almonds
- 1/3 cup salad shrimp
- ½ tablespoon diced cilantro
- 1 package ramen
- 2-3 cups of water

Instructions:

In pot mix oil, onion, garlic, corn, okra, edamame, and almonds.

Sauté vegetables 1-2 minutes.

Add in shrimp, cilantro, thyme, ramen, water.

Bring to boil, reduce heat, cover, let simmer 8-9 minutes.

Cheesy Ham and Ramen

Try it with Monterey jack cheese! Makes 2 servings

Ingredients:

- 1 package ramen
- 1/3 cup diced ham
- 1/3 cup diced chicken
- ¼ cup trinity mix
- 2 basil leaves sliced
- ½ teaspoon parsley diced
- 1 cup shredded cheddar cheese
- ½ cups low sodium chicken broth

Instructions:

In pot mix ramen, ham, chicken, trinity mix, broth.

Bring to a boil, reduce heat, cover, let simmer 5-7 minutes.

Top with herbs and cheese before serving.

Queso with Chicken Ramen

Try adding chipotle peppers! Makes 2 servings.

Ingredients:

- 1 package ramen
- 1 Tbsp olive oil
- 1 shallot diced
- 1/2 tsp minced garlic
- 1/3 cup shredded chicken
- 1 Tbsp tomato sauce
- 1/3 teaspoon chili powder
- 1/4 teaspoon cumin
- ½ Tbsp cilantro (optional)
- 1 cup shredded mozzarella cheese or queso melting cheese

Instructions:

In a pot add oil, onion, garlic; sauté 2 minutes.

Add in shredded chicken, tomato sauce, chili powder, cumin.

Make a bed of ramen and ladle chicken and sauce on top.

Top with cheese.

Ramen Steak and Broccoli

Also, great with sweet ginger turmeric! Makes 2 servings

Ingredients:

- 2 Tbsp diced onion
- 1 clove grated garlic
- 1 cup stir-fry strip flank steak
- ¼ cup chopped red peppers
- ¼ cup diced parsley
- 2 tablespoon low sodium soy sauce
- 1 teaspoon sesame oil
- 2/3 teaspoon pepper
- 1 teaspoon ginger
- 1 package ramen
- 3 cups beef broth

Instructions:

In pot sauté onion, garlic, peppers 1 minute.

Add in steak, parsley, soy sauce, sesame oil, pepper, red pepper flakes, ramen, broth.

Bring to a boil, reduce heat, cover, let simmer 8-9 minutes.

Artic Ranch Ramen with Andouille

Serve with crunchy bread and good wine! Makes 2 servings

Ingredients:

- ½ cup diced onion
- 1/3 cup diced green bell pepper
- 2/3 cup diced andouille
- 1 8 oz. can no salt added tomato sauce
- 1 packet ranch seasoning
- 1 package ramen
- 5 cups low sodium chicken broth
- 1 Tbsp diced cilantro (optional)
- 2 cups shredded Monterey jack cheese or habanero cheddar

Instructions:

In a pot over med-high heat sauté onion and bell peppers 1 minute.

Add in andouille and cook 30 seconds.

Stir in tomatoes, ranch seasoning, ramen, broth, cilantro.

Bring to a boil, reduce heat, cover, let simmer 8-9 minutes.

Divide between two bowls and top each with cheese.

Southern Stew

For protein try adding beans, ground pork, tofu, or fish! Makes 2 servings

Ingredients:

- ¾ tsp minced garlic
- 1 Tbsp grated onion
- 1 cup diced eggplant
- ¼ cup diced scallion
- 1 cup chopped cabbage
- 1/2 teaspoon paprika
- 1 package ramen
- 3-4 cups low sodium vegetable or beef broth

Instructions:

In a pot sauté onions and garlic 1 minute.

Add in eggplant, scallions, cabbage and cook 1 minute.

Add in ramen, broth.

Bring to boil, reduce heat, cover, let simmer 6-8 minutes.

Ramen Ragu

A hit with kids! Makes 2 servings.

Ingredients:

- 2 cups ground beef, browned
- ½ tsp Italian seasoning
- 8 oz. tomato sauce
- 1 tablespoon dry white wine
- 3-4 cups low sodium beef broth
- 1 cup chicken or beef broth
- 1 package ramen
- 1 cup shredded mozzarella or sharp white cheddar

Instructions:

In pot combine ground beef, seasoning, tomato sauce, white wine, broth.

Bring to boil, stirring constantly, reduce heat, cover, and let simmer 5-10 minutes, stirring frequently.

Divide ramen between two plates and top with hot mixture.

Top with cheese.

Creamy Chicken Ramen

Serve with crunchy Italian bread! Makes 2 servings

Ingredients:

- ¼ cup onions, julienned
- 1 tsp minced garlic
- 1 spoonful chicken flavored bouillon paste (we used Better Than Bouillon Chicken)
- 2 cups shredded chicken
- 1 can low sodium condensed cream of chicken soup
- 1 tsp Italian seasoning
- 1 can low sodium veggie mix (peas, carrots, corn, potatoes, lima beans, etc.)
- 1 package ramen
- 1 cup low sodium chicken broth
- Shredded mozzarella and provolone cheese (optional)

Instructions:

In Dutch oven sauté onions and garlic 1 minute.

Whisk in bouillon paste, add in shredded chicken and cook 1 minute.

Stir in condensed soup, seasoning, veggie mix, ramen, broth.

Bring to boil, reduce heat, cover, let simmer 5-10 minutes.

Chicken Mojo Ramen

Big flavor in no time! Makes 2 servings.

Ingredients:

- ½ diced onion
- 1 teaspoon minced garlic
- 3 chopped jalapenos
- 1 cup diced leftover chicken
- 2 cups low sodium mojo liquid marinade
- ½ teaspoon pepper
- 1 Tbsp chopped parsley
- 1 package ramen

Instructions:

Marinade chicken in mojo marinade for 10 minutes.

In pot sauté onions, garlic, and peppers for 2 minutes.

Dump marinade and put chicken in pot.

Toss in black pepper, parsley, and ramen.

Black Bean and Tomato on a Bed of Ramen

Also good with chickpeas! Makes 2 servings

Ingredients:

- 1 package ramen, cooked
- ½ cup ground sirloin, browned and drained
- 1 can low sodium black beans, wash and drained
- 1 cup diced fresh tomatoes
- 3 sliced basil leaves
- 1/4 Tbsp diced thyme
- ½ tsp red pepper flakes
- 1/4 cup extra virgin olive oil

Instructions:

Divide ramen between two plates and flatten with back of spoon.

Drain burger and return to pot.

Mix ground sirloin, beans, tomatoes, basil, thyme, red pepper flakes, oil.

Top each serving of ramen with half of mixture.

Turkey Ramen Stew

Also, great with pork! Makes 2 serving.

Ingredients:

- 1/3 cup diced mushrooms
- 1/2 tsp minced garlic
- 1 scallion, diced
- 1/3 cup peas and carrots
- 1/2 bell pepper, julienned
- 1/3 onion, julienned
- ½ cup ground turkey, cooked
- 1 cup ramen
- 1 cup beef stock (depends how thick you like your gravy)

Instructions:

In pot combine mushrooms, garlic, scallion, peas and carrots, bell pepper, onion and let sauté 1 minute.

Add in cooked ground turkey, ramen, beef stock.

Cook on 5 minutes.

Vegetarian Ramen Italian Veggies

Try herbs de province! Makes 2 servings

Ingredients:

- 1/2 tablespoon oil
- 1 diced shallot
- 1 tablespoon minced garlic
- 1/3 cup + 1 tbsp mixed vegetables (carrots, green beans, peas, and corn)
- 1 package ramen
- 1 cup vegetable stock
- 1/3 tsp Italian seasoning
- 1/6 tsp nutmeg
- 1/6 tsp cinnamon

Instructions:

Pour oil in pot and sauté onions, garlic, and veggies 2-3 minutes.

Add in ramen, stock, seasoning, nutmeg, cinnamon.

Spicy Italian Sausage Ramen Bowl

Great side! Makes 2 servings

Ingredients:

- 1/2 tablespoon oil
- 1 diced onion
- 1 tablespoon minced garlic
- 2 diced jalapeno OR 1 tsp red pepper flakes
- 1/3 tsp Italian seasoning
- 2 cups spicy Italian sausage
- 1 cup ramen
- 3-4 cups chicken or vegetable stock

Instructions:

In pot sauté onions, garlic, chopped jalapenos 3-5 minutes over oil.

Add in sausage pieces and Italian seasoning. Cook sausage 45 seconds to 1 minute.

Add in ramen and stock.

Bring to a boil, reduce heat, cover and simmer 5-8 minutes.

Kielbasa and Sauerkraut

Great side dish! Makes 2 servings

Ingredients:

- 1/2 tablespoon oil
- 1 diced onion
- 1 tablespoon minced garlic
- 1/3-1/2 cup sauerkraut
- 1-2 cups sliced sodium free kielbasa
- 1 package ramen
- 3-4 cups chicken or vegetable stock

Instructions:

In pot sauté onions, garlic, and sauerkraut.

Add in kielbasa. Cook sausage 45 seconds to 1 minute.

Add in ramen and stock.

Bring to a boil, reduce heat, cover and simmer 5-8 minutes.

Italian Sausage Ramen Bowl

Add in some black beans! Makes 2 servings

Ingredients:

- 1/2 tablespoon oil
- 1 diced onion
- 1 tablespoon minced garlic
- 2 diced jalapeno OR 1 tsp red pepper flakes
- 1/3 tsp Italian seasoning
- 2 cups spicy Italian sausage
- 1 cup ramen
- 3-4 cups chicken or vegetable stock

Instructions:

In pot sauté onions, garlic, chopped jalapenos 3-5 minutes over oil.

Add in sausage pieces and Italian seasoning. Cook sausage 45 seconds to 1 minute.

Add in ramen and stock.

Bring to a boil, reduce heat, cover and simmer 5-8 minutes.

Ramen Kimchi Soup

Try rice noodles! Makes 2 servings

Ingredients:

- 1 cup chicken stock
- ¼ cup purple onions, julienned
- 1 chopped clove of garlic
- 1 tablespoon tomato paste
- 1 cup stew tomatoes
- 1 cup ramen noodles
- 1/3 cup kimchi
- 1 diced parsnip
- 1 teaspoon thyme

Instructions:

In a large pot over medium-high heat and cook the garlic and onions until the onions are golden in appearance.

Add in tomato paste, stewed tomatoes, rice noodles, kimchi, parsnip, thyme.

Slowly pour in the stock. Lastly add the beans.

Bring to a boil and reduce heat; cover and simmer for 40 minutes.

Tomato and Eggplant Ramen

Add in cabbage! Makes 2 servings

Ingredients:

- 1/2 tablespoon olive oil
- 2 cups vegetable stock
- 1/2 cup tomatoes and okra
- ½ cup diced eggplant
- 1/6 teaspoon nutmeg
- 1 teaspoon honey
- 2/3 teaspoon garlic powder
- 1/3 tsp ginger

Instructions:

In Dutch oven over high medium high heat combine oil, stock, tomatoes and okra, eggplant, nutmeg, honey, garlic and ginger.

Let come to a boil then reduce heat to low.

Let simmer 5-10 minutes.

Kimchi with Ramen

Also great with rice noodles! Makes 2 servings

Ingredients:

- 1 Tbsp butter or ghee
- ½ Tbsp olive oil
- ¼ cup caramelized purple onions, julienned
- 2 chopped cloves of garlic
- 1 tablespoon tomato paste
- 1 cup stewed tomatoes
- 1 cup ramen noodles
- 1/3 cup kimchi
- 1 diced parsnip
- ½ tsp diced oregano
- 1 bay leaf
- 1-1 ½ cup chicken broth or stock

Instructions:

In pot over low to medium heat melt butter into oil.

Sauté onions 15-20 minutes.

Add in garlic, paste, tomatoes. Mix

Stir in noodles, kimchi, parsnip, oregano, bay leaf, chicken broth.

Turn up heat to medium high.

Bring to boil, reduce heat, cover, simmer 5-8 minutes.

Remove bay leaf before eating.

Spicy Herb Ramen

Great for herb gardens! Makes 2 servings.

Ingredients:

- 1 tablespoon olive oil
- ¼ cup purple onion, chopped
- ¼ cup worth peppers, bell or Chile
- 1 tsp garlic minced
- 1/2 tsp. dried oregano
- 1/2 tsp. dried thyme
- 4-5 dashes of hot sauce
- 1/3 cup bay scallions, cooked and drained
- 1/3 cup kimchi
- 1/3 cup kale or seaweed
- ½-1 cup ramen noodles, cooked as directed on package
- 2-4 cups vegetable broth or stock

Instructions:

In pot over low to medium heat melt butter into oil.

Sauté onions, garlic, and peppers 3-5 minutes.

Add in oregano, thyme, hot sauce, scallions, kimchi, kale or seaweed, ramen, liquid.

Bring to a boil, reduce heat, cover, simmer 55-10 minutes.

Turkey Stew

Works with chicken or pork too! Makes 2 servings.

Ingredients:

- 1/3 cup onions julienned
- 1 clove chopped garlic
- ½ cup shredded turkey
- ¼ cup peas and carrots
- ¼ cup yellow/wax beans
- ¼-1/3 cup chicken or vegetable stock
- 1 cup ramen

Instructions:

In pot over low to medium heat melt butter into oil.

Sauté onions 3-5 minutes.

Add in garlic and tomatoes. Mix

Stir in noodles, turkey, peas and carrots, beans, chicken or vegetable stock.

Turn up heat to medium high.

Bring to boil, reduce heat, cover, simmer 5-8 minutes.

Onion Soup

Serve with crunchy bread! Makes 2 servings

Ingredients:

- 1 tsp thyme
- ½ tsp black pepper
- 3/4 Tbsp onion soup mix (such as Lipton's)
- 3 Tbsp diced mushrooms
- 3 Tbsp diced celery
- 1 cup ramen noodles
- 2 – 3 cups chicken or vegetable stock

Instructions:

In a large pot add thyme, onion soup mix, mushrooms, celery, ramen, stock.

Let come to a boil then turn heat down to low.

Let simmer 8-10 minutes.

Apple Chops on a Bed of Ramen

Try it with blueberry pie filling! Makes 2 servings

Ingredients:

- 2 bone in pork chops
- 2 cup apple pie filling (sauce, chunks, and all)
- ¼ tsp cinnamon
- 1/6 tsp nutmeg
- 1/2 Tbsp lemon juice
- 2 Tbsp water
- 1 package ramen, cooked separately
- 2 Tbsp chopped parsley

Instructions:

In crockpot add pork chops, apple pie filling, cinnamon, nutmeg, lemon juice, water.

Cook on high 45 minutes – 1 hour.

Make a bed of ramen on both plates and top each with 1 chop and apple pie filling.

If desired, top with parsley.

Pork Carnita on a Bed of Ramen

Mix in some salsa! Makes 2 servings.

Ingredients:

- 1 3-5 lbs. pork shoulder or butt
- 1/3 cup mojo marinade
- ½ Tbsp chopped cilantro
- 1/3 Tbsp chopped oregano
- 1 Tbsp chopped pepperoncini
- ½ tsp black pepper
- ½ tsp lemon peel
- 1/3 tsp sweet paprika
- 1/3 tsp garlic powder
- ¼ tsp onion powder
- 1 package ramen
- 1 Tbsp chopped parsley

Instructions:

In crockpot combine mojo marinade, cilantro, oregano, pepperoncini, black pepper, lemon peel, sweet paprika, garlic powder, onion powder.

Place pork in marinade and cook on high 4-6 hours depending on size.

Serve meat on a bed of ramen and top with parsley.

Beef Carnita on a Bed of Ramen

Who needs a tortilla! Makes 2 servings.

Ingredients:

- 1 3-5 lbs. beef roast
- 5-6 cups beef broth, low sodium
- ½ Tbsp chopped cilantro
- 1/3 Tbsp chopped oregano
- 1 Tbsp chopped pepperoncini
- ½ tsp black pepper
- ½ tsp lemon peel
- 1/3 tsp sweet paprika
- 1/3 tsp garlic powder
- ¼ tsp onion powder
- 1 package ramen
- 1 Tbsp chopped parsley

Instructions:

In crockpot combine broth, cilantro, oregano, pepperoncini, black pepper, lemon peel, sweet paprika, garlic powder, onion powder.

Place meat in marinade and cook on high 4-6 hours depending on size.

Serve meat on a bed of ramen and top with parsley.

Ramen Beef Stew

Fast comfort food! Makes 2 servings.

Ingredients:

- ½ Tbsp olive oil
- ½ tsp beef bouillon paste (we used Better Than Bouillon Beef)
- 1/3 cup julienned onions
- 1/3 tsp minced garlic
- 2 cups stew meat
- 1/3 cup carrots and peas
- ¼ cup sliced potatoes
- 1/3 tsp Italian seasoning
- 1 package ramen
- 2/3 cup beef broth

Instructions:

In pot pour in oil then sauté onions and garlic 1-2 minutes.

Mix in bouillon paste then add in meat and let cook 1-2 minutes per side.

Mix in carrots and peas, potatoes, seasoning, ramen, and broth.

Bring to a boil, reduce heat, cover, simmer 5-8 minutes.

Gluten Free Chicken with Spring Onion Ramen

Gluten, dairy, and wheat free! Makes 2 servings.

Ingredients:

- ½ tsp olive oil
- 1/3 tsp sesame oil
- ½ tsp chicken bouillon paste (we used Better Than Bouillon Beef)
- 1/3 cup julienned onions
- 1/3 tsp minced garlic
- 1/2 cups shredded chicken
- ½ cup chopped Bok choy
- 1/3 cup matchstick carrots
- ¼ cup edamame
- 1/3 tsp whole kernel corn
- 1 package ramen
- 2/3 cup low sodium chicken broth

Instructions:

In pot whisk together oils, chicken bouillon paste.

Add onions, garlic, and sauté 2-3 minutes.

Add in chicken, bok choy, matchstick carrots, edamame, corn, ramen, and broth.

Bring to a boil, reduce heat, cover, simmer 5-10 minutes.

Sauerkraut and Kielbasa

International ramen! Makes 2 servings.

Ingredients:

- ½ Tbsp olive oil
- 1/3 cup julienned onions
- 1/3 tsp minced garlic (optional)
- 1 tsp thyme (optional)
- 1 package sliced kielbasa, cooked as directed
- 1/3 tsp black pepper
- 1 package ramen
- 1/4-/3 cup broth or water

Instructions:

In pot over oil add in onions, garlic, thyme then sauté 2-3 minutes.

Ann in kielbasa, pepper, ramen, and liquid.

Bring to a boil, reduce heat, cover, simmer 5-10 minutes.

Creamy Chicken with Tortillas

Any chips will do! Makes 2 servings.

Ingredients:

- 1 package ramen, made as directed
- Tortilla chips

Instructions:

Make chicken ramen, with seasoning packet as directed.

Mix in whole and crushed tortilla chips.

Easy Chicken Fajita Ramen

Top with cilantro! Makes 2 servings.

Ingredients:

- ½ Tbsp olive oil
- ½ Tbsp chicken bouillon paste
- 2/3 tsp garlic, minced
- ¼ cup fajita onions and peppers
- Ramen noodles
- 1/3 cup chicken shredded
- ½ tsp chili powder
- 1/3 cup diced tomatoes

Instructions:

In a pot add oil, bouillon paste, minced garlic, onions and pepper and sauté 2-3 minutes.

Add in noodles, chicken, chili powder, diced tomatoes.

Bring to a boil, reduce heat, cover, simmer 5-10 minutes.

Ramen Enchilada

Makes a great casserole! Makes 2 servings.

Ingredients:

- ½ Tbsp olive oil
- ½ cup diced onion
- ½ tsp garlic, minced
- 1-2 diced jalapenos (optional)
- 2/3 tsp chili powder
- ½ tsp cumin
- ¼ tsp paprika (smoky or sweet)
- 1/3 cup shredded cheddar cheese
- 2/3 cup no salt tomato sauce
- ½ cup browned drained ground beef
- 1 package ramen, made as directed
- ¼ cup shredded cheddar cheese (optional)
- 1 Tbsp diced parsley (optional)

Instructions:

In pot add oil and sauté onions, garlic, and jalapenos 2-3 minutes.

Add in chili powder, cumin, paprika, cheese, tomato sauce, and burger.

Stir together.

Toss in ramen noodles.

Divide between two plates and top with cheese and parsley.

Salsa Ramen

Great with homemade tortillas! Makes 2 servings

Ingredients:

- ¼ cup salsa (use your fav low sodium variety!)
- ½ cup ground beef, browned and drained
- 1/3 cup worth tortilla strips
- 1/3 tsp chili powder
- 1 package ramen
- 1/3-1/2 cup chicken broth or stock

Instructions:

In pot combine salsa, ground beef, tortilla strips, chili powder, ramen, broth or stock.

Bring to a boil, reduce heat, cover, simmer 5-10 minutes.

Beef Au Jus with Ramen

Great lunch for leftover roast! Makes 2 servings.

Ingredients:

- ½ cup shredded roast beef
- ½ Tbsp olive oil
- 1/3 cup julienned onions
- ½-2/3 cup au jus condensed soup
- ¼ cup chopped mushrooms
- 1 package ramen

Instructions:

In pot combine oil, onions, and mushrooms.

Sauté 2-3 minutes.

Stir in beef, condensed au jus, and ramen.

Bring to a boil, reduce heat, cover, simmer 5-10 minutes.

Chicken Ramen Soup

Add in peppers or mushrooms! Makes 2 servings

Ingredients:

- 1/2 Tbsp olive oil
- ½ tsp minced garlic
- 1-2 cups frozen stir-fry veggies(thawed)
- ½ cup shredded chicken
- 1 bay leaf
- ½ tsp Italian seasoning
- 1 package ramen
- 2-3 cups chicken broth or stock

Instructions:

In pot combine oil, onions, and garlic.

Sauté 2-3 minutes.

Stir in veggies, chicken, Italian seasoning, bay leaf, ramen, broth.

Bring to a boil, reduce heat, cover, simmer 5-10 minutes.

Peppers and Ginger Ramen

Add in some basil and black beans! Makes 2 servings.

Ingredients:

- ½ Tbsp olive oil
- 1/3 cup diced spring onion
- ½ tsp garlic, minced
- 2 julienned red bell peppers
- 1/3 tsp ginger
- ½ tsp cumin
- ¼ tsp paprika (smoky or sweet)
- 1 cup chicken or vegetable broth
- 2 Tbsp grated parmesan, divided

Instructions:

In a pot combine oil, garlic, onion, peppers, ginger, cumin, and paprika.

Bring to a boil, reduce heat, cover, simmer 5-10 minutes.

Greek Ramen

Simply delicious! Makes 2 servings.

Ingredients:

- 2/3 cup no salt tomato sauce
- ½ cup browned drained ground beef
- 1 package ramen, made as directed
- 1/2 Tbsp Greek seasoning
- ½ cup beef broth or stock
- 1/3 cup cheese crumbled feta, divided

Instructions:

Cook ramen as directed and divide between two plates.

In a pot combine tomato sauce, ground beef, ramen, seasoning, broth/stock.

Bring to a boil, reduce heat, cover, simmer 5-10 minutes.

Cod Ramen

Good with all types of proteins! Makes 2 servings.

Ingredients:

- ½ Tbsp olive oil
- ½ cup diced onion
- ½ tsp garlic, minced
- 1-2 diced jalapenos
- 2/3 tsp beau monde spice
- 1 can gluten free cream of chicken soup
- 1 cup sliced cod, browned

Instructions:

In pot combine oil, garlic, jalapeno and sauté 2-3 minutes.

Ramen with Scallops

Great with shrimp too! Makes 2 servings.

Ingredients:

- ½ Tbsp olive oil
- ½ Tbsp grated red onion
- ½ tsp garlic powder with parsley
- 1/3 tsp smoked paprika
- ½ cup scallops
- 1 package ramen, made as directed
- 1 Tbsp diced parsley (optional)
- ½-2/3 cup tomato ginger broth or stock

Instructions:

In pot combine oil, onions, garlic powder, paprika and sauté 1 minute.

Add in tomato sauce, scallops, ramen, broth/stock.

Bring to a boil, reduce heat, cover, simmer 5-10 minutes.

Hot Smoky Shrimp Ramen

Also, great with scallops! Makes 2 servings.

Ingredients:

- ½ Tbsp olive oil
- ½ cup diced onion
- ½ tsp garlic, minced
- 1/2 tsp jalapeno powder
- 1/3 tsp red pepper flakes
- ¼ tsp smoked paprika
- ¼ cup diced shrimp
- 1 package ramen, cooked as directed

Instructions:

In pot combine olive oil, onion, and garlic.

Sauté 1 minute.

Add in jalapeno powder, red pepper flakes, paprika, shrimp.

Sauté 1 minute.

Toss in ramen and serve!

Italian Ramen Ragu

Also, try it with chicken! Makes 2 servings.

Ingredients:

- ½ Tbsp olive oil
- ½ tsp garlic powder
- 1/3 cup shredded cheddar cheese
- 1/3 cup + 1 Tbsp no salt crushed tomatoes
- ½ cup browned drained ground beef
- 1 package ramen, made as directed
- ¼ tsp Italian seasoning
- 1 cup beef broth
- 1/2 Tbsp diced thyme for topping

Instructions:

In pot combine oil, garlic powder, cheese, tomatoes, ground beef, seasoning, broth.

Bring to a boil, reduce heat, cover, simmer 5-10 minutes.

Author's Afterthoughts

Thanks ever so much to each of my cherished readers for investing the time to read this book!

I know you could have picked from many other books, but you chose this one. So, a big thanks for reading all the way to the end. If you enjoyed this book or received value from it, I'd like to ask you for a favor. Please take a few minutes to **post an honest and heartfelt review on** *Amazon.com.* Your support does make a difference and helps to benefit other people.

Thanks!

Julia Chiles

Printed in Great Britain
by Amazon